Published by Creative Education
123 South Broad Street, Mankato, Minnesota 56001
Creative Education is an imprint of The Creative Company

Art direction by Rita Marshall
Production design by The Design Lab

Photographs by Corbis (Bettmann Archive, Steve Raymer), Department of Defense,
Tom Myers Photography, North Wind Picture Archive, U.S. Army, U.S. Navy, Unicorn
Stock Photos (Karen Holsinger Mullen, A. Ramey), West Point Military Academy

Library of Congress Cataloging-in-Publication Data

Fandel, Jennifer.
The military / by Jennifer Fandel.
p. cm. — (Let's investigate)
Summary: Introduces the United States military forces,
their purposes, and what it is like to serve in the military.
ISBN 1-58341-264-6
1. United States—Armed Forces—Juvenile literature.
[1. United States—Armed Forces.] I. Title. II. Series.
UA23.F345   2003
355'.00973—dc21   2002034864

First edition

2   4   6   8   9   7   5   3   1

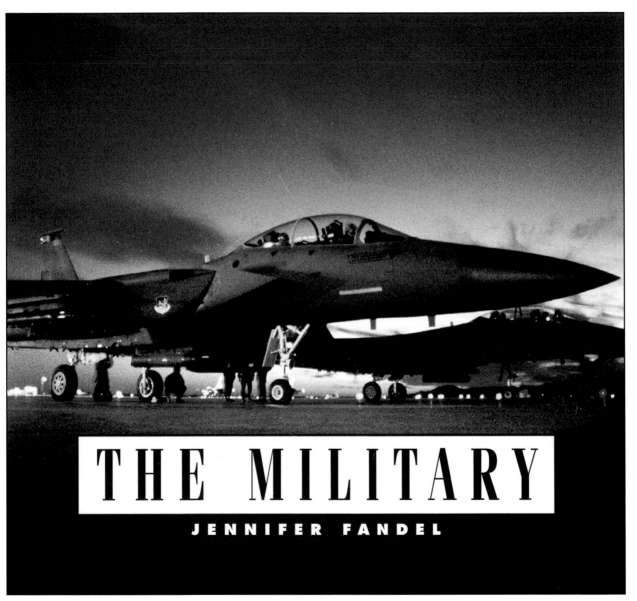

THE MILITARY

JENNIFER FANDEL

Education

MILITARY
COMMAND

The president of the United States is the commander in chief of the military. All of America's military commanders answer to the president.

Above, a president greeting officers Right, Army troops in formation

The United States military has a long and proud history. From its early days to the present, its mission has always been to protect the land and people of America. The U.S. military has been victorious in 10 of the 11 major wars in which it has fought—failing to win only in the Vietnam War—and is known around the world for its strength.

MILITARY

The first air force in U.S. history took to the skies around 1860, when soldiers floated hot-air balloons to spot the enemy during the Civil War.

6

Above, a Civil War spy balloon
Right, an 18th-century recruitment poster

Before the United States became its own, independent nation, American **colonists** had their own military. Colonists put together local volunteer military forces called **militias**. These militias were sometimes called into action to fight hostile Native Americans.

TO ALL BRAVE, HEALTHY, ABLE BODIED, AND WELL DISPOSED YOUNG MEN, IN THIS NEIGHBOURHOOD, WHO HAVE ANY INCLINATION TO JOIN THE TROOPS, NOW RAISING UNDER GENERAL WASHINGTON, FOR THE DEFENCE OF THE LIBERTIES AND INDEPENDENCE OF THE UNITED STATES, Against the hostile defigns of foreign enemies,

TAKE NOTICE,

GOD SAVE THE UNITED STATES.

An illustration of Americans fighting the British in the Revolutionary War

When American colonists fought against the ruling British in the Revolutionary War (1775–1783), many militias banded together against the enemy. Men between the ages of 16 and 60 joined their local militias and encouraged others to serve. Each man who served in a militia was required to provide his own weapon and receive occasional training. It was from this tradition of volunteer service that the modern American military took form.

The Army, Navy, and Marine Corps were all founded in 1775, a year before the U.S. proclaimed its independence from Britain. The Army was founded first, and its job was to protect American lands and waterways. Later that year, Americans decided that they needed a separate sea force. The Navy was then created, followed soon after by the Marines. Because air and space technology developed much later, the Air Force is the youngest division of the military. The Air Force was officially born in 1947. Before that time, aircraft troops were considered part of the Army.

MILITARY
POWER

The U.S. Congress has the power to declare war when necessary. The Congress also determines how much money is spent on the military.

9

MILITARY

G U N S

The 21-gun salute is the highest military tribute. It is reserved for national holidays, ceremonies welcoming foreign dignitaries, and funerals for presidents.

A military squad firing a 21-gun salute

MILITARY POWER

The Army, Navy, Air Force, and Marine Corps are the four main branches of the military, also called the armed forces or armed services. Each military branch focuses on different areas of **defense**. The individual forces usually train and work separately, yet they may share equipment or join together to fight as a **unified** force during times of war.

The Blue Angels and the Thunderbirds are two military flying groups that perform for spectators in events throughout the United States.

11

Above, the Thunderbirds fighter jets (F-16s) Left, a loaded aircraft carrier at sea

T he Army is known as a ground force. Its members, called soldiers, fight battles on land using both close-range and long-range weapons such as rifles and missiles. Soldiers may also be trained to drive humvees (jeeps) or tanks, and some may fly airplanes and helicopters. The Navy is a sea force whose members, called seamen, usually fight battles with ships and submarines. The Navy also has its own pilots who fly aircraft from huge ships called aircraft carriers.

The Marine Corps is the smallest of the military's main branches. Its members, called marines, are the only military troops trained to fight on land, in the air, and at sea. The Marine Corps often acts as an **amphibious** force, moving from the sea onto land during battle. Marines may be supported by the Air Force. Members of this armed force, called airmen, defend America using air and space technology such as fighter jets and **satellites**.

12

Marines are versatile troops that use an array of equipment, including jets

MILITARY
T I M E

The military does not divide the 24 hours of the day by A.M. and P.M. It counts by hours 100 through 2400 instead. So 3:00 P.M. in military time is called 1500 hours.

The U.S. is often referred to as a superpower because it has by far the most powerful military in the world. There are many factors behind this strength. The U.S. is a large and wealthy country that spends a lot of money training and equipping its armed forces. The country also spends a lot of money on the development of technology. This means that the military is provided with the newest and best weapons, communication systems, computers, and other equipment.

Army soldiers manning a satellite communications station

14

The education of the U.S. population is another reason for America's great military might. All citizens are required to attend school through high school, and many people go on to receive college degrees. Some men and women attend military colleges and universities, such as the Air Force Academy, the Military Academy at West Point, and the United States Naval Academy (for both the Navy and the Marine Corps). These schools emphasize military strategy, international politics, and history, preparing students to become military officers.

Soldiers and marines may learn to use computer-guided weapons

Early in America's history, the nation's first president—George Washington—had trouble getting men to **enlist** as soldiers during peacetime. Worried that America would be vulnerable in the event of a sudden attack, President Washington made a law that let the government **draft** men into the military in times of war.

MILITARY
UNIFORM

For a long time in America's early history, the Army dress code was not enforced because the government did not have enough money to buy a new coat for every soldier.

15

President George Washington helped to build up America's armed forces

MILITARY
NUMBERS

In 2001, the U.S. military included about 1.4 million men and women on active duty. These forces were supported by an additional one million troops in the reserve forces and the National Guard.

A group of students in the Reserve Officers Training Corps (ROTC)

This practice continued throughout much of U.S. history but was stopped in 1973 after the Vietnam War. The Selective Service System was then developed, requiring young men to register their names with the government when they turned 18. In an emergency, this program allows the government to easily locate men to fill out the military's ranks if enlistment is low.

Since the end of the Vietnam War, the U.S. has had an all-volunteer military. Men and women interested

in military service may be **recruited** at the age of 18. Many young adults see the military as a great opportunity to see the world, earn money for college, and learn valuable skills for the workforce. Some people who wish to go to college and train for military service at the same time join the Reserve Officers Training Corps (ROTC). Through this program, students become officers in the military after graduating college. They are then required to spend six to eight years on active duty or in reserve forces.

MILITARY TAGS

Members of the armed forces sent into combat wear identification tags around their necks. These have been nicknamed "dog tags."

Above, a stamped metal "dog tag"

MILITARY
COLOR

During combat, soldiers wear fatigues—earth-colored clothes designed to help them blend into their surroundings so they are not easily spotted by the enemy.

MILITARY
DECORATION

*Each member of the military has a dress uniform that he or she wears for special occasions. The uniform may be decorated with patches and medals that explain the person's **rank** and any honorable duties he or she has performed.*

National Guard troops delivering relief supplies after a hurricane

Men and women can also become members of the National Guard or the Reserves. These are part-time troops that can be called up for active duty in times of emergency. Reserve troops are put on active duty during national emergencies, while the National Guard can be activated for either national or state emergencies. Governors oversee their state's National Guard and can call its troops to duty when natural disasters such as floods or hurricanes occur or when riots and conflicts break out.

During Army boot camp, men must be able to do 17 sit-ups and run a mile (1.6 km) in 8 minutes and 30 seconds. Women must be able to do 17 sit-ups and run a mile (1.6 km) in 10 minutes and 30 seconds.

19

"BASIC" AND BEYOND

All new military recruits are required to attend basic training, also known as boot camp, at one of the many **military bases** in the U.S. Each branch of the service runs its own basic training sessions, which last from 6 to 12 weeks. This training period makes new recruits stronger and helps prepare them for any situations they may face if they are sent into combat.

Above, boot camp recruits on a run Left, recruits enduring the intensity of "basic"

MILITARY
H A I R

When male recruits enter basic training, they receive a very short, or shaved, haircut. This makes all of the men look the same, emphasizing the importance of unity.

Above, a seaman getting a military haircut
Right, an Army boot camp instructor

In boot camp, recruits exercise, march, and practice using weapons. They are also put through tough physical and mental challenges, such as **obstacle courses** intended to build confidence and endurance, and **battle simulations** to test their skills and reactions in battle. Through these challenges, the recruits learn to rely on one another and to work as a team.

After passing the rigors of boot camp, every soldier, marine, and airman attends a training course to learn a specific military skill. Recruits are placed in a program that develops each person's unique talents. Members of the military may receive training as mechanics, foreign language interpreters, computer or communication specialists, cooks, or engineers, to name a few programs. Navy sailors may also receive such skill training, but more often they go to their first ship assignment to receive on-the-job training.

The U.S. military is working to develop identification tags that store important information, such as a person's medical history, on tiny computer parts called microchips.

21

Military mechanics working on a Navy aircraft's engine

MILITARY
BRAVERY

The Medal of Honor is a medal given to men and women who show bravery in combat that is considered above and beyond the normal call of duty.

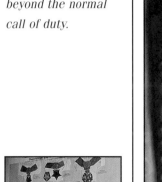

*Above, military medals
Right, a special forces
captain receiving a
medal for valor*

Military personnel may receive promotions throughout their service and move up in rank. Although each branch of the armed forces has its own system of rank, the branches are similar in structure. Highly ranked officers usually command and supervise, while lower-ranked personnel usually prepare for and fight in battles. Typically, a new recruit in the Army, Air

Force, or Marine Corps starts as a private and may move up in rank to become a corporal, sergeant, warrant officer, lieutenant, captain, major, colonel, or general. The Navy has a similar ranking system that calls new recruits seamen and top officers admirals.

MILITARY
MEDAL

The Purple Heart is a medal awarded to those who are wounded in battle. The medal is considered a great honor.

24

MILITARY LIFE

Life in the military is based on order and **discipline**. Members of the armed forces are expected to abide by strict rules of conduct. Everyone on a military base rises early in the morning and must follow set schedules for such activities as showering, eating, exercising, and even relaxing. All personnel are expected to maintain a neat appearance as well. That means having their boots polished, their beds made, and their lockers well-organized at all times.

Marine recruits preparing for inspection during basic training

MILITARY EXPERTS

The Green Berets and the Navy Seals are two of the military's special forces. These small forces, made up of America's best soldiers, get sent on especially difficult missions.

MILITARY MONUMENT

The Tomb of the Unknown Soldier, located in Arlington National Cemetery, is a monument honoring all unidentified soldiers who were killed in combat.

All men and women in the service must be respectful of their commanders and obey their orders. They must also show respect by raising their right hand in a salute when they greet anyone of a higher rank. Members of the armed forces are required to work when and where their superiors say.

Members of the elite Green Berets in salute

MILITARY

MISSING

Some soldiers have never returned home from war, yet no one knows what happened to them. These soldiers are called MIAs: those who are Missing In Action.

MILITARY

HARDSHIP

Soldiers who are captured by the enemy during war are called POWs, or Prisoners Of War.

A U.S. Air Force base on the Pacific island of Guam

Members of the armed forces are **stationed** at military bases all over the world. They are often transferred to new locations every two or three years. Military bases are set up like small communities and are equipped with stores and services that provide almost everything a person might need. Bases have their own doctors, nurses, cooks, janitors, secretaries, and chaplains (religious leaders who offer worship services and spiritual guidance). All of these jobs are

usually staffed by people in the service. Even though most of these jobs are not as dangerous as being a foot soldier or a fighter pilot, they are all important. Every one of these jobs helps the military function properly.

One of the most difficult things about serving in the military is being away from home. Writing letters to friends and family and attending worship services can help keep up spirits.

Above, Navy sailors celebrating Christmas at sea

MILITARY

W O M E N

Women are allowed to pilot combat aircraft and serve on most ships, but they are not allowed to serve in ground combat units.

MILITARY

FAIRNESS

In 1948, U.S. President Harry S. Truman passed a desegregation order, giving African-Americans in the military the right to train and live side-by-side with white military personnel.

MILITARY CHANGES

Women and minorities have been part of the U.S. military for most of its history, but they were not always treated fairly or recognized for their achievements. The face of the military has changed greatly from its early days. Women, African-Americans, Latin-Americans, and other minorities now serve in larger numbers, and many have earned high honors and ranks. Looking at today's military, one sees a more accurate reflection of the American population.

A group of female Air Force officers having completed pilot training

The mission of the U.S. military has also changed. While its first goal is still to protect the people and land of America, it also serves a larger purpose throughout the world. Many countries look to the U.S. for help because it has so much power. The military's muscle and expertise are used for combat when necessary, but more often the armed forces are called upon for peacekeeping and assistance in parts of the world suffering the effects of war and natural disasters. The skill and power of the military make it a force that can adapt to many situations.

MILITARY
M E A L S

Soldiers in combat are issued MREs, which means Meals, Ready to Eat. These dehydrated, light-weight, and easy-to-carry food items were once called C-rations, or combat rations.

Above, soldiers eating MREs Left, a U.S. soldier on a peacekeeping mission in war-torn Bosnia

MILITARY
MEMORIAL

Memorial Day, May 30, is a national holiday to honor and remember the men and women of the military who died serving their country.

MILITARY
TRIBUTE

People who have served in the armed forces are called veterans. The U.S. honors these individuals with a national holiday called Veteran's Day, which is celebrated on November 11.

Hardworking people and top technology give the military its strength

Few militaries in the world can claim the record of success earned by the U.S. armed forces. Throughout American history, brave men and women have felt a call to duty and have responded by fighting for their country. Through hard work and sacrifice, members of America's Army, Navy, Air Force, and Marine Corps help to uphold freedom around the world.

Glossary

Being on **active duty** means working for the military on a full-time basis.

An **amphibious** military force is one that fights on both land and water.

Battle simulations are pretend battles that test how soldiers will act during combat.

Colonists were people from Europe who settled in the 13 colonies (British-controlled areas) of the United States before it was an independent country.

A country's **defense** is the means it uses to fight off enemies and protect itself.

To show **discipline** is to follow set rules and behave in an appropriate way.

To **draft** people into the military is to order them to serve.

People who **enlist** in the military are those who sign up, or volunteer, for duty.

Military bases are large, security-guarded areas where military personnel live, work, and train.

Militias are small, armed groups that organize themselves to fight for a cause.

Obstacle courses are challenging races over rugged land that may include running, jumping, climbing, and crawling.

A person's position in the military, such as private, sergeant, or general, is called his or her **rank**.

A person who is encouraged to join the military is said to be **recruited**. A newly recruited person is called a recruit.

Satellites are objects that fly in space and can send information down to Earth through advanced technology.

When a member of the military is sent to a specific place for a set amount of time, he or she is **stationed** there.

When people work together toward a common goal, their work is said to be **unified**.

Index